ART ON THE GO

ACRYLIC

STYLES AND TECHNIQUES

First published in 2011 by
SpiceBox™
12171 Horseshoe Way
Richmond, BC
www.spicebox.ca

Text Copyright © 2011
SpiceBox™

ISBN 10: 1-926905-66-0

ISBN 13: 978-1-926905-66-2

CEO and Publisher: Ben Lotfi
Editor: Trisha Pope
Creative Director: Garett Chan
Art Director: Christine Covert
Designer: Leslie Irvine
Production: James Badger
Sourcing: Janny Lam

Book illustrations: Bill Diggins and Mona Malekian
Photography: Alan Roberts

Printed in China

CONTENTS

INTRODUCTION

Left: Acrylic paints are opaque, which makes them easy to work with.

Acrylics are a wonderful modern painting medium, a by-product of the plastics industry. They are simple to work with, produce brilliant colors, and display a versatility that allows you to create many beautiful effects. With acrylics, you can replicate the rich, burnished glow of oil paints, the delicate transparency of watercolors, and everything in between. So don't be afraid to experiment—another advantage is that it's easy to correct mistakes in acrylics.

The most important thing about acrylics is their versatility. You can use them straight from the tube to get a thick, opaque effect. Or you can water them down for a thin, transparent effect, which allows you to build up a painting in layers to create rich colors and textures.

Remember when working that acrylics dry rapidly. If you want a blurred watercolor look, work quickly and apply new layers on still-wet paint. However, for most techniques, you should let paint dry before applying the next layer—a positive bonus for this quick-drying medium.

*Above: Thinning acrylics with water makes them
almost transparent, like watercolors.*

ARTIST'S MATERIALS

There are some basic supplies that you will need to start painting in acrylics. You will want to have a basic range of brushes, a palette and a palette knife, as well as a supply of paints. The color choices are vast, but if you start with these colors, you will find you can mix almost all the tones you are ever likely to require:

- White–thick, bright white
- Lemon yellow–cool yellow
- Vermilion–warm orangish red
- Crimson–cool scarlet red
- Burnt sienna–rich warm brown
- Viridian–dark cool green
- Ultramarine–warm pure blue
- Prussian blue–cool greenish blue, also called phthalocyanine blue

You may eventually want to add a warm yellow ochre, a fresh sap green, a clear purple, and possibly black.

Lemon yellow, white, ultramarine, and viridian

Vermilion, crimson, prussian blue, and burnt sienna

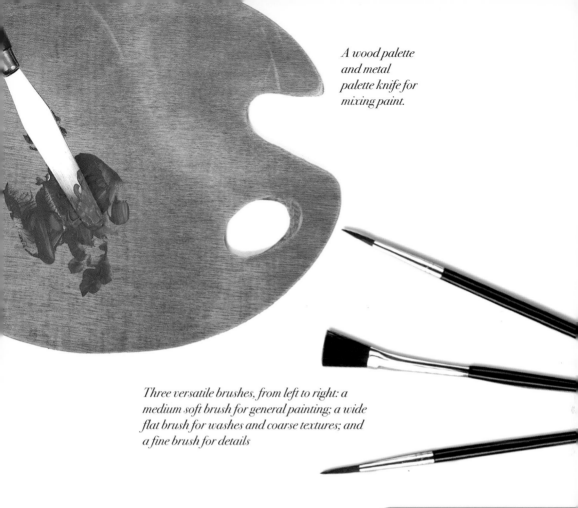

A wood palette and metal palette knife for mixing paint.

Three versatile brushes, from left to right: a medium soft brush for general painting; a wide flat brush for washes and coarse textures; and a fine brush for details

Exploring mediums

Mediums are liquids, gels, and pastes you can add to acrylics to boost their potential. Some increase transparency and drying time, while others give a gloss finish.

- If you choose just one, a heavy gel medium is the best choice. It bulks up paint and gives it body, so it is good for impasto and knife painting. It also makes your paint go further.

- Mixing paint with any of the mediums makes it look lighter than it will when it dries on the page. Always read the label on the jar before using.

Technique Tip
Extra brushes and tools
Increase the effects you can achieve by obtaining a coarse hogshair brush for thick paint, a large soft brush for washes, a blunt-ended brush for stippling, and a metal palette knife for knife painting.

COLOR MIXING

One of the joys of painting in acrylics is the quality of the colors. Their vivacity, purity, and ease of use are in many ways unsurpassed by other mediums, which makes them a good way to learn about and experiment with color. There are a few principles that apply to all color. If you understand them, you will be better prepared to move beyond the ready-made paints that are available in tubes and to mix the myriad of subtle, nuanced colors you see in the world around you.

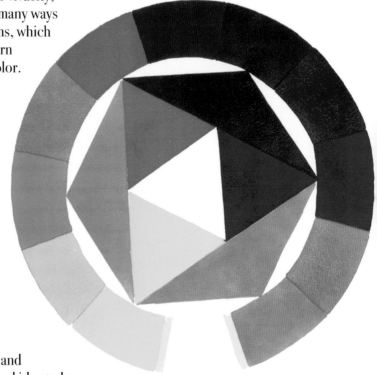

Warm and cool colors
Most colors come in "warm" and "cool" versions, and it is a good idea to have both in your painting kit for color mixing.

| *Warm yellow* | *Cool yellow* | *Warm red* | *Cool red* | *Warm blue* | *Cool blue* |

• See also Artist's Materials, and Opaque and Transparent Techniques

The color wheel

A color wheel (left) gives a graphic picture of how colors relate to and are made from each other.

- The primary colors form the inner triangle and are the colors from which all the others are made.

- The secondary colors form the middle section and are made from mixing equal parts of two adjacent primary colors. So blue and yellow (primaries) make green (secondary).

- The tertiary colors—yellow-green, yellow-orange, red-orange, violet-red, violet-blue, and blue-green—are made by mixing equal amounts of a primary and a secondary color. Together with the primary and secondary colors, they form the outer circle of the color wheel.

Adding water

Though not strictly color mixing, most colors can be lightened by adding water (above). The more watery the paint, the more the paper or base coat will show through and the less intense the color will appear.

Adding white or black

Colors may be lightened by adding white to them, as well as darkened by adding black (above). But there are some important things to remember when using either of these colors:

- White acrylic is opaque, so the lightened color will be milky and never truly transparent. Some colors change their character when white is added to them.

So, while lightened blue and yellow remain true to their nature, red changes to pink when only a very little white is added to it.

- Some artists feel that adding black to darken a color deadens it. Instead add some of its complementary color to make it deeper (see page 11).

Primary colors
Colors that cannot be made by mixing other colors are known as primaries—these colors are red, yellow, and blue. Remember that these colors come in both warm and cool versions.

Secondary colors
Colors that are created by mixing two primary colors are known as secondaries— these colors are orange, green, and violet. To create bright secondaries, choose two primaries with the same degree of warmth. Mixtures across the warm-cool divide can produce muted, more subtle colors. If you want a warm, vivid orange, mix crimson (warm red) with yellow ochre (warm yellow). If you want a cool, bright green, mix prussian blue (cool blue) with lemon yellow (cool yellow).

Complementary colors

Colors opposite each other on the color wheel are known as complementaries— the secondary color green is the complementary of the primary color red; violet is the complementary of yellow; orange is the complementary of blue; and so on right down to the most subtle mixes. These pairs of colors have a special affinity for each other and are very effective when used together.

The complementary colors shown here are primary and secondary colors, but all colors have their complements—for example, red-orange is the complement of blue-green.

- Painting a color next to its complementary will have the effect of "throwing forward" the lighter color. So yellow painted on a violet background will stand out more than it would if painted against green.

- Painting a color next to its complementary will make the two colors seem to "dance" against each other. For example, red next to green or orange next to blue can be used to produce energy and tension in a picture and will have an enlivening, even jarring effect.

- Adding its complementary to a color is a good way to darken it without dulling it. Adding a little blue to darken orange, or green to darken red, is better than adding black and produces a more vibrant color.

BRUSH ACTION

It may seem obvious, but many painters forget the importance of brush strokes. Good brushwork makes a painting look more dynamic and interesting, and it can communicate the "essence" of an object. Acrylic paint holds brush marks very well.

Coarse bristle brushes are good for rough effects such as impasto.

The handle of a brush dipped in thick paint produces large dots.

A flat brush makes broad strokes, applying wide slabs of color. The same brush used upright gives fine lines.

Right brush, right stroke

Explore the versatility of your brushes, and try variations using the tip and side of the same brush. The marks they make will bring to mind appropriate uses—wispy strokes for grasses, chunky strokes for heavy or dominant shapes, or smooth, watery strokes for skies and backgrounds. The amount of paint you load on your brush will also make a big difference to the effects you can achieve.

A round brush applied with light pressure delivers a thick, rounded shape. The tip produces fine lines.

Dabbing on color with a fairly dry, blunt-ended brush creates an effect called stippling.

Suggesting form

Look for ways to use brush strokes freely in a way that suits what you are painting. Do not be content simply to apply color flatly within a given shape.

- A confident stroke following the contour of a rounded object such as an apple will make it seem rounder and heavier.

- A wavy stroke would be a natural way to depict furrows in a field or reflections in a pool of water.

- Flat, heavy strokes mimic bricks or stone when used to paint buildings. Use fine, wispy strokes for grasses or hair.

- Learn to be economical with your brushwork, too—a single, deft stroke can suggest a leaf or branch of a tree better than a painstakingly accurate rendition.

In the project Barcelona Square, broad textured strokes applied in dollops recreate the feeling of dappled sunlight.

• See also Broken Color, Dry Brush, and Scumbling

Technique Tip
How to avoid "blobs" of paint

Start by using your brush to lay out small quantities of the color needed, as acrylics are very fast-drying. If a blob of paint has started to dry, peel off this "skin" to avoid shreds of the rubbery color being brushed into wet paint. Once a blob has fully dried, removing it will peel off part of your picture.

In the project Marshland with Poppies, angled wispy strokes in different colors depict grasses against the broad, horizontal strokes of the fields behind.

15

OPAQUE TECHNIQUES

Most acrylic paints are opaque, which simply means that you cannot see through them in the way that you can transparent or translucent paints such as watercolors. For this reason, as with oil painting, most acrylic painting is done in layers, each one covering the layer beneath to a greater or lesser extent depending on the techniques used.

Painting in layers has distinct advantages. It means that there is always the chance to overpaint errors. Acrylic is a fast-drying medium so colors can be readjusted cleanly and there is no risk of muddying colors already put down. Dark paint can be used over light paint, and light paint will cover dark paint. All this gives enormous flexibility and room for experiment.

When painting with opaque colors, think about the areas you want to stand out and paint them last. Because they will not be covered with subsequent layers, they will dominate the picture, especially if they are warm colors that naturally come forward.

Things to consider

- Color that is thinned with only a little water will still give a smooth opaque finish.

- Only one or two colors may not be completely opaque—experiment to see—but these can be made opaque by adding a little white paint or another opaque color.

- White paint is totally opaque and when increasingly mixed with color will reduce the intensity of that color.

- If thick acrylic paint is used it will not crack but will leave visible brush marks when dry.

- Opaque acrylics will dry with a sheen.

- Acrylics dry slightly darker than they appear when wet—the pigment is suspended in a medium that is white when wet, but colorless when dry. This is not normally a problem but may be a concern when matching colors.

• See also Broken Color, Scumbling, Impasto, Knife Painting, and Extruded Paint

Painting light over dark

The beach scene (previous spread) uses opaque techniques in different ways. First the blue sky, green sea, and golden sand are laid down and allowed to dry. Then darker opaque colors are splattered onto the sand and brushed over the sea to give texture and depth. Finally, the white birds and waves are added, completely obscuring the layer beneath to conjure up the solid form of the birds, or letting some background color show through to give movement to the foaming waves.

Painting in layers

For the beach huts (right), the artist started by painting the sky in three layers—the mid-blue background, lighter blue strokes over that, finishing with darker blue strokes. The white areas were left unpainted. The reds and yellows came last, their clean outlines and warm colors dominating the painting.

Technique Tip
Don't ruin your brushes
Never let paint dry out on your brushes. Acrylic dries quickly, and if brushes get caked with paint, they will be ruined: There is no rescue remedy. Regularly wash out your brushes in clean water— have more than one jar on hand.

Start by painting the blues and greens: cool colors that recede. Overpaint with yellows, oranges and reds: warm colors that advance.

19

TRANSPARENT TECHNIQUES

Though naturally opaque, acrylic paint can be thinned with water to make transparent washes of color, resembling watercolor painting. As a first step, a transparent wash applied as an underpainting to an entire picture unifies the composition, providing a useful background.

A transparent color applied over still-damp paint will bleed and blend into it, to achieve a subtle and expressive mixture of color called wet-into-wet.

Because acrylics dry rapidly and are permanently fixed once dry, you must work quickly to achieve this effect.

But as a transparent wash applied over dry paint, acrylic paint really comes into its own. Known as glazing, it will transform the color beneath, burnishing and enriching it with a veil of translucent color and creating very beautiful effects not possible in any other medium. The dry layers are permanent, so they will not be lifted or muddied by subsequent transparent layers, only enhanced.

Worth remembering
- Thin washes of acrylic will dry with a matte finish.
- Layering thin washes of acrylic paint works best on textured paper.
- Thin washes of acrylic paint are good for correcting mistakes in watercolor painting.

• See also Wet-into-Wet and Glazing

For reflections on still water, paint a thin wash all over and, before it dries, make a few horizontal strokes roughly following the inverted image.

Wet and dry effects

For the trees and water in the scene at left, the bottom layer of paint was still wet when the next layer was applied—notice how the colors look thin and hazy, and the way they all blur together. The overall effect is loose and sketchy.

The trees and water above right were created with similarly colored washes of transparent paint, but this time each layer was dry before the next one was applied. Note how the colors are more vibrant and how much more solid the forms of the trees appear.

Use thin color to paint a stand of trees (above), then see where you can apply more layers of transparent color to differentiate one tree from another.

On the water surface, look for pattern-making qualities in the reflections. Keep to a limited palette of three or four tones. To achieve a loose, sketchy feeling, you will have to develop an almost abstract approach to resolving the painting.

Technique Tip
Keep your paints wet
On your palette, acrylics need to be kept moist to keep the paint from forming a plastic skin. Occasionally spray the palette with water, and keep it sealed in a plastic bag when not working. On your paper, you can also keep paints wet and therefore workable for longer by spraying lightly with water.

21

BUILDING UP

The best way to work in acrylics is to take an overview of the whole painting and loosely block in the main shapes, tones, and colors. Then proceed in the traditional way of building up from light to dark, adding highlights at the end.

Although it is perfectly possible with acrylics to paint a thin wash over a thickly applied color, it is unlikely that a flat area can be achieved—obvious brush or knife marks will show through as a texture.

Underpainting and colored grounds

• Underpainting is the practice of laying down the main tonal areas of a painting in a neutral color, which is then built upon for a final, rich effect. The color must blend with the finished painting as some of the underpainting will show through.

• A colored ground is an overall thinned wash of a neutral tint such as gray, gray-blue, or earthy brown. It helps unify a composition, especially if some of it is allowed to show through in the finished picture. It also provides a contrast for highlights. Against this ground, white will appear lighter, and stronger tones will be darker and more vivid.

Underpainting allows you to establish the light and dark tones of a composition and then build up color in successive layers.

22

Helpful hints for working in layers

- Laying down a colored ground may help you set the mood for a painting. Many artists find it less daunting than starting out with a stark white page.

- Build up the picture as a whole. Avoid taking one part of the picture to a high degree of finish too soon.

- Try to work with a larger brush for as long as possible. The constant use of small brushes will result in a tight, overworked, fussy picture.

- Remember that in acrylics you can overpaint with lighter colors at any time in the painting process. This allows you not only to correct mistakes but to build up interesting color effects, layer by layer.

• See also Opaque and Transparent Techniques, and Glazing

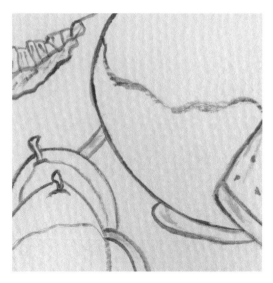

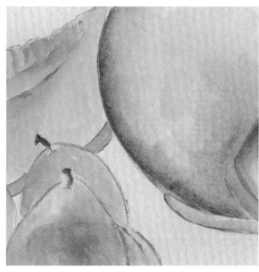

1. Start by making an outline drawing of the whole composition, working with a medium brush in a neutral color.

2. Next, block in large areas, starting with backgrounds and minor features. Don't worry about detail now.

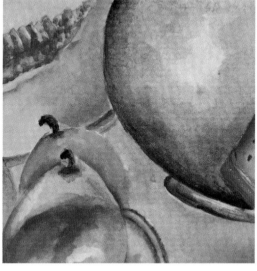

3. Continue by building up dominant areas of the picture, introducing warmer tones and defining shapes.

4. Finish by overpainting additional layers of color, especially the fine details and highlights.

WORKING WITH COLOR

The skill of blending colors on the painted surface—as opposed to on your palette—is one of the most important techniques to understand and to master. Using color is, after all, the way you create the impression of reality. With color you can define an object and give it form; with color you can give the illusion of depth and perspective, of vitality and movement. Layers of applied color also allows you to build up a jewel-like richness on the surface of your painting. Acrylics are sometimes unfairly criticized for giving a hard-edged, unblended appearance, largely because of their quick-drying quality. But there are several techniques you can use to blend colors successfully. The studies on the right demonstrate how effectively they can be used, separately or together.

Ways of blending colors

- Glazing (1) involves building up several transparent or semitransparent layers of color over dry underpainting to give a luminous and rich depth of color. Color mixed in this way is one of the distinctive and very beautiful effects of painting in acrylics.

- Broken color (2) produces a mottled effect by placing distinct brush strokes next to each other. It gives a lively impression, full of movement. Both dry brush and scumbling are related to broken-color techniques, using either brush action or the texture of the paper to break up the paint surface.

- Dry brush (3) is the act of dragging a fairly dry brush loaded with a small amount of color over the painting surface so that the paper or color beneath is only partly covered. It can involve transparent or opaque paint.

- Painting wet-into-wet (4) is typically a watercolor technique in which transparent or opaque paint is stroked over or dabbed into wet paint or paper. The colors diffuse and merge into each other on the paper, producing a hazy blend without any hard edges.

- Scumbling (5) is a kind of dry brush technique in which a brush load of color is scrubbed over the surface, allowing the base color to show through to produce an uneven effect.

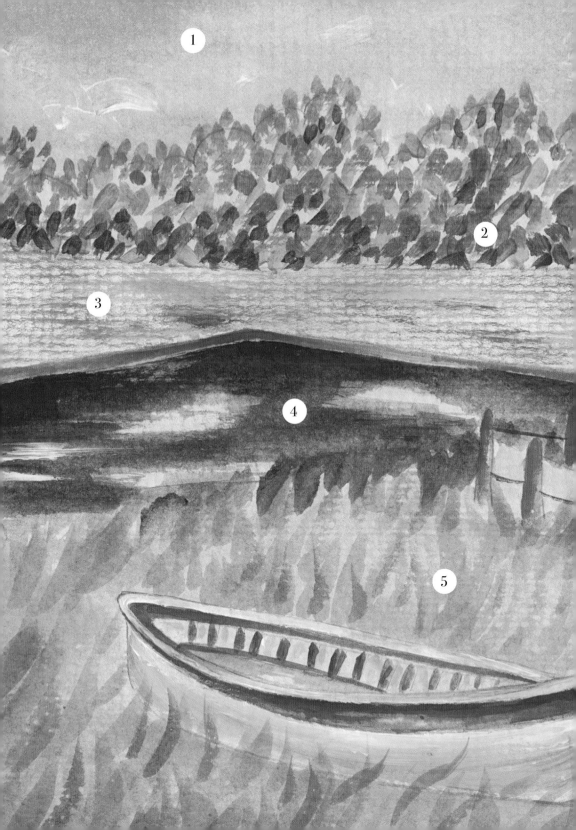

WET-INTO-WET

Working wet-into-wet is a lovely technique in which wet colors are brushed or dropped into each other so that they blend on the page, without leaving any hard, visible edges. You can, in theory, paint with acrylics in this way, but it can be tricky as the paints dry so fast. So work as speedily as you can, and spray your work and your palette with water from time to time to keep the paints moist. Another trick is to work on wet paper, which does not dry out so quickly. You can also add a substance to the paint, called a retarding medium, which slows the drying process.

Painting skies

Wet-into-wet is the ideal technique for painting almost all weather conditions, especially skies and other misty atmospheres. Useful colors to draw on include ultramarine, burnt sienna, lemon yellow and, if you have them, yellow ochre, and umber.

Stormy sky

Thick wet-into-wet paint with soft blurred edges gives the effect of an imminent storm.

Use thick paint in ultramarine, yellow ochre, and umber on dry paper. Paint freely with a wet brush, using very little water. Make sure that all the colors go down separately but overlap when they are still wet. Use vigorous brush strokes and keep the blending of colors to a minimum.

• See also Artist's Materials and Transparent Techniques

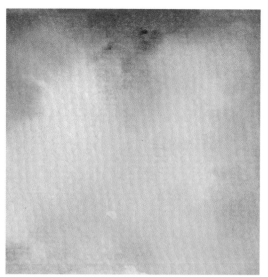

Low cloud (left)

Leave the center of the cloud white to suggest electrically charged low cumulus clouds scudding across the sky, driven by a strong wind.

Saturate the surface with clear water. While this is still wet, pick up a diluted mix of ultramarine and make some swirling brush strokes toward the top of the shape. Without cleaning the brush, add a few touches of a second blue. Beneath the white cloud a little umber will give the impression of shadow.

High cloud (right)

Here the lines of color simulate the high cirrus cloud known as a "mackerel sky."

Paint a wash of thin yellow ochre and allow this to dry. Once dry, flood the area with clear water and, while it is still wet, make a few thin parallel lines of ultramarine and umber.

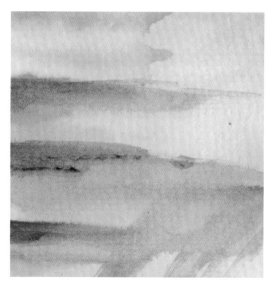

Watery sunlight (left)

Pale, thin washes of color perfectly convey the sky on days when even the sun looks wet.

On wet paper, lay a wash of thin lemon yellow. Run horizontal brush strokes of thin wet ultramarine and burnt sienna, making sure to leave a circle of yellow wash showing. Allow the colors to dry before adding diagonal washes of the same colors to reveal shafts of sunlight.

GLAZING

Glazing is a "transparent technique" in which a thin film of paint is applied over an underlying color, beautifully transforming it while at the same time allowing some of it to show through. It is another way besides painting wet-into-wet to blend colors on the page rather than on the palette. Also, by building up several veils of color, you will give the painted surface a rich depth. Glazing is an ideal way of handling delicate and subtle variations of color and tone when portrait or figure painting.

This lovely effect is a hallmark of painting in acrylics. And as a glaze can only be painted over dry paint, it is particularly suited to this fast-drying medium.

How to mix and use glazes

- Prepare a glaze by making a thin mix of color and water that will dry to a dull matte finish.

- Greater depth and transparency to a glaze may be achieved by adding a gloss or matte medium to the paint. If a gloss medium is used, it will dry with a slight sheen.

- Some colors are more transparent than others when reduced with water. It is always worthwhile experimenting by making some test swatches of color on a separate piece of paper.

- For the most vibrant effects, work from light to dark, as a dark over a light color will have more impact.

- Paler colors can, however, be glazed over darker colors to create a translucent glow. Glazing with very thin white paint creates an attractive misty effect, but remember that white acrylic is essentially opaque.

Painting dark over light can create a third color.

Painting light over dark gives a bloom to the base color.

Technique Tip
Emphasizing texture

A thin color glaze stroked over a rough impasto base will adhere to the low spots of the surface but not to the peaks, giving an even more pronounced textured effect as well as enriching the color.

Thin glazes of deep red over warm red enhance the color and shape of the apple, while a white glaze creates important highlights. A second wash of the same pale green used for the table is all that was used to create the apple's shadow. A very thin white glaze washed over the blue background gives it a milky glow.

BROKEN COLOR

When distinct strokes of paint are laid alongside each other rather than being graded or blended seamlessly, this is a technique—pioneered by the Impressionists—known as broken color. From a distance, marks of different colors can appear to merge as one, a phenomenon known as optical mixing, which creates a very vibrant effect. Only tonally similar colors merge well.

Broken color usually employs opaque paints. Build up separate strokes over an underpainted flat area or a colored ground, or apply geometric dots of unmixed color with the end of a brush handle. Use a combination of dashes, dots, squiggles, and swirls.

Technique Tip
Practice with pattern
Make brush marks on a sheet of clear plastic, then place it over an area of flat color. Make more patterns of color on other sheets of plastic and experiment with overlapping them.

• See also Brush Action

Dynamic effects

Broken color literally pulsates on the page, creating
an impression of vitality and movement. Bright colors,
swirling shapes, diagonal compositions, dappled light, and
reflective surfaces all suit this technique.

DRY BRUSH

Dry brush is a surface effect that creates a broken, dragged texture. The process calls for comparatively more color and less water on the brush, so take off any excess water with a piece of paper towel or rag every time you pick up more paint.

The texture of the painting surface is also an essential part of the dry brush technique. If paint is dragged across a surface that has a coarse grain, color will not seep into the indentations, leaving the characteristic broken effect.

You can use either thick paint with a stiff bristle brush or thin paint with a soft, square-ended or fan-shaped brush. Spread out the brush hairs and then gently stroke the painting surface. You will be able to see the brush marks.

Dry brush technique allows unpainted paper to show through (below).

This technique also lets you see contrasting, underlying colors (right).

• See also Scumbling

Some natural effects you can achieve

Dry brush is perfect for simulating the textures and patterns found in nature. It creates a very free and spontaneous impression of complexity and movement, of light dappled through the leaf canopy or playing on water. These effects can all be achieved with a few deft strokes. Avoid going over your strokes unnecessarily, however, or you will spoil the effect.

Fur—use delicate colors and short strokes.

Windblown grass—make very free, wispy strokes.

Tree bark—use both the tip and side of a brush to add depth and texture.

Highlights on water—in a single stroke, drag a light color over darker blues to simulate light reflected on water.

Technique Tip
A textured surface
If you are painting on smooth paper, a little fine sand or sawdust added to a base coat will provide a good roughened surface ideal for dry brushing over.

SCUMBLING

Scumbling or scrubbing an uneven layer of paint over a completely dry existing color will add texture and interest to a work. The paint is applied with a fairly stiff, dry brush in a light, rhythmic, circular motion, using thick paint, though thinner paint may be used so long as the brush is not too wet. Successive layers may be in a contrasting or similar color, depending on how subtle or dramatic the desired result. Scumbling is an impressive method of painting, but one that is difficult to restrict to a small area.

Keys to success

- The most important thing to remember about scumbling paint is not to cover the underlying color completely.

- As with the related dry brush technique, keep only a limited amount of water on the brush.

- Maintain a flowing, continuous movement of the brush, and change from one color to another without rinsing the brush in water.

- As you proceed, think of mixing colors on the painting surface, as if it were the palette.

- Skim over the surface in a loose and spontaneous way. Let the texture of the paper or the underlying layer of paint help you.

Scumbling darker tones over the same color lends texture and form to objects, helping them to appear more three-dimensional.

• See also Broken Color and Dry Brush

Technique Tip
Hands on
Scumbling is an instinctive way to work. Paint may be applied with a large brush, a stiff rag, or even the tips of your fingers.

WORKING WITH TEXTURE

Using different textures is an underexploited area of painting, yet the techniques are simple and fun to do. Many of them do not even involve using a brush. Just think about how best to communicate the physical presence of the object you are depicting—textured effects work especially well for subjects in nature such as rocks and bark—and be as creative and innovative as you like. There are no rules!

Acrylics are unrivaled in their ability to create interesting textures. They hold brush marks and other shapes well and can be bulked up with a medium to make them thicker and more malleable. The painting on the right shows how different textures can be used to communicate the physical sensations and excitement of a day at the beach—just think how different the picture would feel if all the surfaces were perfectly smooth.

Interesting surface effects

- Splattering (5) and sponging (3) create the illusion of texture by means of tiny dots of splattered paint or the abstract patterns a natural sponge makes as it presses color onto the painted surface. These techniques are also sometimes used to blend colors.

- Sgraffito (2) describes the act of scratching lines or other marks into the top layer of paint, scraping it away to reveal the layer beneath. It gives energy to the painted surface and can be very exciting.

- Impasto (4) is thick paint applied to the surface of a painting so that the brush marks and lines can be clearly seen. It tends to emphasize and bring forward the part of the picture where it is used.

- Knife painting (1) is an exaggerated form of impasto, in which the paint is laid on with a knife, forming stiff peaks and other dramatic shapes. The 3-D effect is very bold and eye-catching.

SPLATTERING AND SPONGING

Irregular flecks of paint may be used to depict textures from nature, such as crumbling stone, or to enliven flat color. These techniques add spontaneity, texture, and pattern to your work, but a little goes a long way so avoid overdoing them.

Sponging is often used to lend interest to backgrounds, while splattering and flicking are typically added at the last minute. Flicked and splattered paint is difficult to control, so mask off any areas of your painting you do not wish to cover. Protect nearby surfaces since acrylics are difficult to remove once dry. Always rinse your brush, toothbrush, or sponge in clear water immediately after use.

Splattering
Splattering suggests pebbles on a beach, windblown spray, and falling snow. The paint needs to be mixed to a milky consistency. Dip the bristles of a toothbrush in the color mix, and with the handle of a paintbrush carefully draw the bristles toward you, directing the splatter where you want it on the painting surface. For a variation, try dropping alcohol onto wet paint with a toothbrush or eyedropper to get random shapes and effects.

Splattering can be done with opaque or transparent paint, on a wet (above) or dry background.

*White flicks are used in the project
Marshland with Poppies to depict
thick grasses in the foreground.*

Flicking

Flicking can portray grasses and other
plants. It is similar to splattering in the
explosive way the paint is applied, but the
marks are more like rods than dots. Load
the end of your brush handle with paint,
hold it over your painting with the handle
pointing in the direction you want the paint
to fall, and flick it briskly. While you have
paint on the end of your brush, you can also
use it to make small dots.

*For the abstract examples, the
colors below are worked in the
same order, starting with yellow.*

Sponging

Sponging with thick, white paint is effective
for portraying churning, foaming water,
while smudges of transparent paint conjure
up atmospheric skies. Sponges large or
small, coarse or fine-textured, natural or
man-made may be used to impress paint
onto the painting surface. Experiment
with the amount of paint, pressure, and
movement you use.

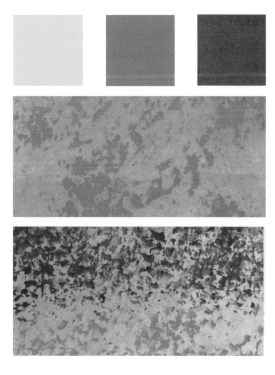

*Sponging can create a crisp texture (right) if
successive layers are left to dry, or a more muted
effect (above) if all the layers are worked wet.*

MASKING

Masking tape is a very useful painting aid. Applied judiciously to the surface of a picture while you work, it will prevent paint from going where you do not want it. This is especially helpful for energetic, unpredictable techniques such as splattering, sponging, and scumbling. When you have finished with that technique, you can remove the tape and continue painting.

Masking without fears

• Position the tape on the painting surface so that it defines a hard edge or shape. The edge does not have to be straight; you can pleat or cut the tape to follow a curve.

• Also use masking tape to secure pieces of scrap paper over large areas you wish to leave unpainted.

• Pieces of paper with torn edges can be secured to the surface of a painting and used as a stencil to create free shapes.

• When painting, if possible try to brush paint away from the tape edge, not toward it, to avoid forcing paint under the tape.

• You can use masking tape equally well on paper or canvas. Only if the surface is too heavily textured is the paint likely to seep under the tape.

• Remove tape with care. If the painting surface seems fragile or likely to be damaged, use a solvent such as lighter fluid, which will ease removal without leaving a stain. Work in a well-ventilated area when using solvents and treat flammable liquids with due care.

Tear a paper strip and tape in place to make a loose edge where the waves ebb and flow on the beach (above).

Use masking fluid to protect paper while splattering the sand (above top). Remove the fluid to expose paper (above center), then paint in shell.

Technique Tip
Sticky situations
To reduce the tackiness of tape and make it easier to remove, hold a piece stretched between both hands. Then, on the edge of a table or work surface, lay the sticky side down and press and release it several times.

Other masking aids
Art masking fluid—a liquid latex solution—can be painted on the paper surface to protect it from paint, then rubbed off to expose the bare paper beneath. It is ideal for making small, irregular, or complex shapes. Use only old brushes or a dipping pen to apply.

• See also Wet-into-Wet, Splattering and Sponging, and Scumbling

SGRAFFITO

The term sgraffito comes from an Italian word meaning "to scratch." This technique involves scoring the painted surface to reveal the color or bare surface beneath. It is a broken color effect that adds texture and pattern to a painting, and marks can be made with either a sharp or a blunt instrument.

The paint must be scored while it is still wet, so it is essential to work quickly with fast-drying acrylic paint. However, acrylics can be mixed with a retarding medium to keep them wet longer. The marks you make will depend on the consistency of the paint and the tools that you use. It is important to plan the position of the underlying layers carefully so that you know what colors will be revealed.

Making your mark

- To make fine, crisp lines, scratch into a fairly thin layer of color with the point of a sharp knife.

- To make furrows or less-defined lines, scratch into thick, wet paint with a blunt implement.

- Make multiple lines by scratching through wet paint with the serrated edge of a knife or the teeth of a hair comb.

- No specific painting aids are available for this technique, so be inventive. Use chopsticks, matchsticks, toothpicks, half an old charge card, or anything else you think will make an intriguing pattern.

Technique Tip

Cut to the quick
If working on watercolor paper, scratch off both color and paper with a sharp craft knife to create highlights. This is a severe step that will damage the paper, but it may give the work an added sparkle.

Teeth of a hair comb

Blunt end of a paint brush

Serrated edge of a bread knife

Point of a sharp knife

IMPASTO

The term impasto derives from the Italian word for "paste," and that's exactly what it is like: a thick, juicy paint used to give strong presence and a three-dimensional quality to a painting. Impasto is a bold, expressive technique. The paint stands upon the picture surface, and the characteristic marks left by the brush, knife, or other implement used to apply the paint add a rich, textural effect.

Paints and brushes

- Make your paint smooth and malleable; mix it and move it around with a palette knife.

- To bulk out the paint, you can add a substance to the paint called an impasto medium. This will increase the volume of the paint, its gloss and transparency, without reducing the intensity of the color.

- Stiff bristle brushes, traditionally used for oil painting, are also just right for impasto acrylic. Their toughness is ideally suited to the application of heavy, coarse paint. Thick acrylic can be quite resistant and needs brushing thoroughly to avoid transferring lumpy textured color onto the working surface.

- Use fingers to apply impasto for simple, effective results.

- See also Artist's Materials and Brush Action

Technique Tip
Get the right color
If you use an impasto medium, mix your color before you add it. Though it dries clear, the medium is white while wet, so it may make your colors appear lighter.

Impasto effects

Broad swathes of thick impasto have a stronger impact than the more restrained layers of scumbling or glazing. Textured paint tends to come forward in a picture, so it may be best to restrict it to the foreground and reserve flatter paint for the recessive background.

Glazing over dried impasto enhances its textured appearance. The rough surface "takes" the glaze only in the depressed areas, not the raised peaks, adding subtlety and depth.

The thickly painted eggs appear heavier and more dominant than they would if flatly painted.

Highlights in white impasto have double the impact, as they do on both the eggs and the sardine tin.

KNIFE PAINTING AND SCRAPING

Paint applied with a knife is an impasto technique in which thick slabs of paint form highly textured ridges and other patterns that catch the light and give a painting an interesting surface. Scraping is a similar technique that produces flatter, thinner layers of paint that cover a wider area.

Knife painting requires thick, opaque acrylic. This form of painting encourages a bold approach, such as the direct method called allaprima, in which markings are made without a preliminary drawing or underpainting. First impressions are put down spontaneously, and the painting is completed in one session.

Scraping can employ thick or thin paint, and transparent layers can be skimmed over opaque color.

Special tools and materials
- For knife painting you will need a special knife. They come in a range of shapes and sizes, including pear-shaped, long, straight and trowel-like ones.

- Use a knife with a raised handle, which will keep your hand clear of the painting surface.

- For scraping, use any one of a variety of straight edges, from a wallpaper scraper to a small piece of stiff cardboard.

- Though it is possible to use acrylics straight from the tube, your paints will go further if you add an impasto medium to bulk them up.

Knife strokes

Use the knife to press paint onto the picture surface and create a flat plane. Where the stroke ends, a ridge forms.

Use the flat edge of a broad knife and lift it repeatedly from the sticky surface to raise a lot of little peaks. Use the tip of the knife to make fine lines and striations.

• See also Impasto

51

EXTRUDED PAINT

Another very satisfying way of applying paint is by squeezing or extruding it straight onto the painted surface. This produces a bold, raised, sculptural texture that is especially effective in conveying strength and energy.

As with other textured techniques, thick, opaque color is mixed to the right hue and then bulked out with an impasto medium. This will also keep the paint moist enough to work for longer than straight acrylics.

Extruded paint may be employed to outline shapes or to create abstract patterns of lines, squiggles, or dots. It can be used over the entire surface of the painting or confined to specific areas. It is best to work on an underpainted design, as mistakes are not easy to correct or paint over.

Technique Tip
A light touch
Do not let the end of your applicator touch the painted surface or you may smear the lines and create unsightly blobs.

• See also Impasto and Knife Painting

Squeezing the paint

Squeezing acrylic paint straight from the tube would seem an easy option, but this delivers the paint very thickly and with an unstable line. To gain more control, use a dropper or a nozzle with a squeeze bag.

To make your own, use a small plastic bag, twist it to force the paint down to the bottom, then neatly snip a tiny hole in one corner for the paint to come out. Or make a small funnel from tracing paper. With a little practice, you will be able to deliver a fine line of extruded paint.

1. Make an underpainting of the image in opaque colors.

2. Use extruded paint to build up raised outlines around the flower shapes.

3. Squeeze thick paint into the areas within the outlines and brush out.

SCALING UP

The easiest way to copy or enlarge a drawing or painting is by marking a grid over the original work and then using it to transfer a copy, square by square, to the new surface. This technique was used for the large studio oil paintings of the Renaissance, where a small sketch by the master artist was scaled up by his assistants onto a canvas many times the size of the original drawing.

All you need is a ruler, a try-square, and a little patience. Once both grids are in place, carefully observe where important lines fall within each square of the original work, then copy them as faithfully as you can within the squares of the new grid. Dealing with one square at a time is obviously a much easier proposition than tackling an entire composition at once.

Enlarging the outline drawings
The outline drawings on pages 56 to 61 will allow you to enlarge any of the project paintings to whatever size you desire. Follow this simple procedure:

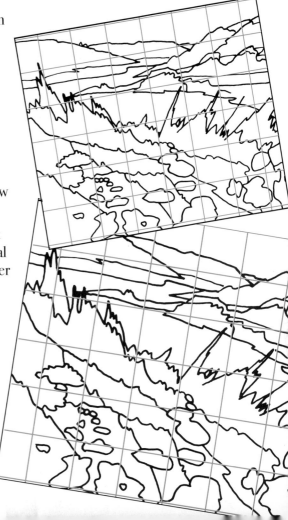

- Draw a grid on your painting surface that is correspondingly larger than the original grid. Make sure you have the same number of squares.

- Use a light pencil for the enlarged grid. For your enlarged drawing use a pencil that is dark enough not to become obscured by any underpainting but light enough so that it will not show through in the finished painting.

Copying an original artwork

The same principles apply if you wish to copy another artwork—from a book or magazine, for example—or a sketch you have previously made. You may enlarge or reduce it as you see fit.

- Draw a grid for the work you are copying. If the original artwork is small enough, make a photocopy and draw your grid right on top of that. Otherwise, use tracing paper or a sheet of clear plastic.

- Use a light pencil for the new grid. You may wish to sketch in your copy by underpainting in a light, neutral shade of paint. This will have the advantage of blending in to the final painting and also giving you a tonal background on which to work.

LESSON ONE
Barcelona Square

LESSON TWO
Summer Irises

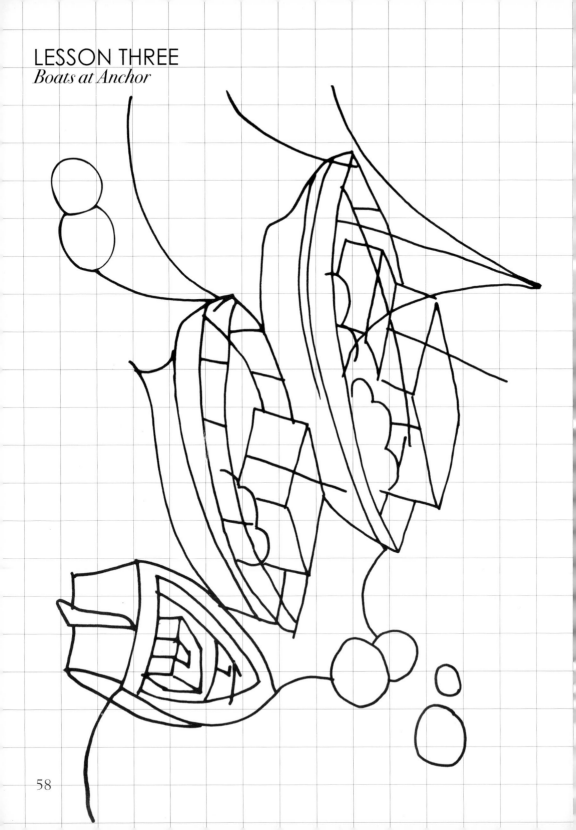

LESSON FOUR
Rooster Romp

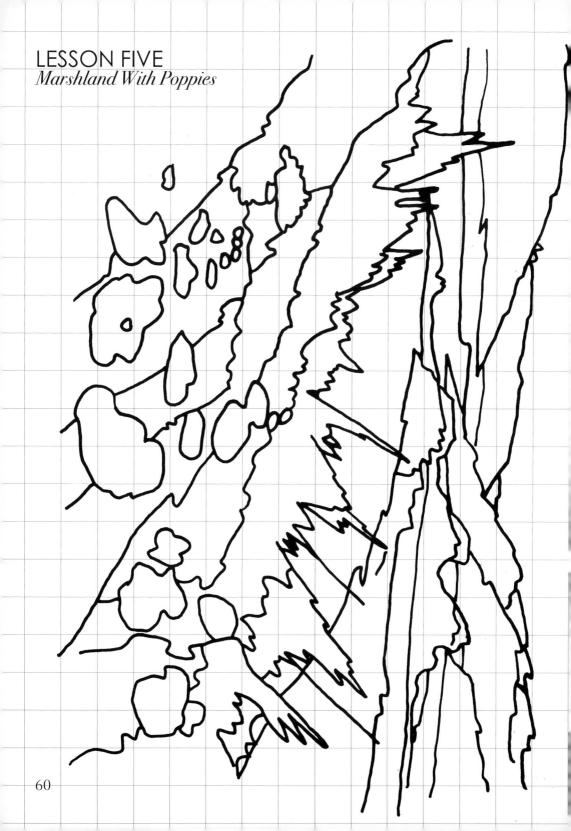

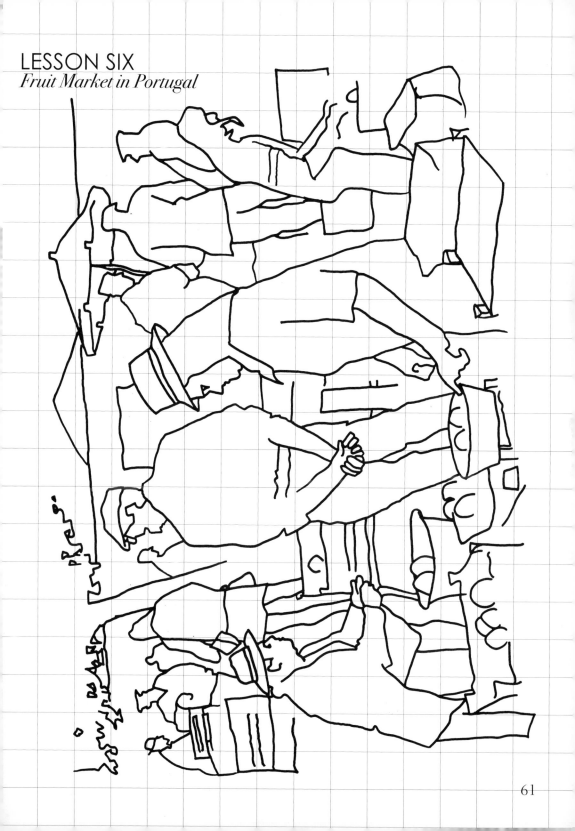

FRAMING AND DISPLAYING

Framing serves both an aesthetic purpose and a practical one—it protects the image and displays your work in the best possible way. Bear in mind, though, that the picture is the center of interest—the frame is only there to enhance the work.

Consider what type of frame is suitable for your picture. A simple surround of plain wood always looks handsome. A deep, carved frame gives your work real presence, while a plain glass frame makes the picture the star.

If you have a cardboard mount, choose a color that complements your picture. Classic white or pastel looks good with most images, while dark mounts are stunning with light pictures. If you cut your own, the golden rule is: Measure twice, cut once! Cut a mount so that the bottom is slightly deeper than the sides or top; this corrects the optical illusion that the picture is lower in the frame than it should be.

Technique Tip
Decorated frames and mounts
Paint a frame with acrylics to coordinate with your picture or continue it into the surround. Mounts can also be trimmed with fine lines, simple designs, or motifs. Look in thrift stores or flea markets for old frames you can clean up and repaint.